To Speak in Volumes

Lauren Kaeli Baker

Copyright © 2021 by A.B.Baird Publishing
All rights reserved. This book or any portion thereof may not be reproduced or used in any manner whatsoever without the express written permission of the publisher except for the use of brief quotations in a book review.

Printed in the United States of America
First Printing, 2021
ISBN 978-1-949321-27-2

All writings within this book belong to the author.
Cover Design by: Austie M. Baird

A.B.Baird Publishing
66548 Highway 203
La Grande OR, 97850
USA
www.abbairdpublishing.com

Catalogue

File me somewhere and make a note
so your fingers can find me by heart
with midnight clarity
reading all my secrets like scripture
like confessions
your eyes colour my words like a sunset

Run your thumb down my spine
and draw comforts in my margins
carry me through neighbourhoods
of anguish and broken promises

My voice is soft but I am learning
how to speak in volumes
I'm learning to be at home
in the dustiest corners of the shelf
I'm learning to be okay whether closed
or wide open

My Volumes (Table of Contents)

Volume I: Latin	Pages 1-12
Volume II: Memory	Pages 13-33
Volume III: Hearts and Hurts	Pages 35-55
Volume IV: Mind	Pages 57-70
Volume V: Twenty Twenty	Pages 71-90
Volume VI: The After	Pages 91-104
Volume VII: The Blackout	Pages 105-114
Gratitude	Pages 115-116
Author Information	Page 117

Volume I: Latin

Apricus

She is:

    Sunshine vessel
gaping window flooding
room

    the warmth of happy
moments and full box of
memory

    dust particle illuminate
fragments of forget

She is:

    Daybreak hope and promise
barefoot and brimming with
light

Lux Brumalis

Lux Brumalis kisses me crisp
      ice crystal flower petals
            frosted mouth to numb cheek

She flavours my thoughts
      mulled wine sipped candlelight
            chocolate dipped tangerine

She breathes down my neck
      soft exhale of glaciers
            avalanche of affection

Lux Brumalis whispers to me
      eerie yellow skies
            silent snowfall on rooftops

                  She knows I'm hers.
                                alone

Solis Occasum

Sunset drapes itself across landscape
dusky pink scarf of silk flung over old lamp
like in the old days

I wonder, can you taste the orange on your tongue
like I can
on yours, I mean.
It tastes sweet and secret like the ones
we used to pull from laden boughs in those
forgotten fields where the sun doesn't go
anymore
It makes me salivate

here, next to you
I feel ripe as those oranges dyed pink
by this sky, layers peeled back before
the death of day

if you wanted I would let you
devour me

Ad Astra per Aspera

She breathes
fills lungs with light
a barefoot pilgrimage
she walks through hardships to the stars
and sings

Auribus Teneo Lupum

I do not flinch, and hold the wolf by its ears
I know that at any moment it could bite
But the beast itself embodies all my fears
It's the thing that bares its teeth to me at night
And yet its pelt is soft between my fingers
I can see myself reflected in its eye
And though a certain wariness still lingers
We have found some common ground, the wolf and I

Meliora

That day I found a four leaf clover
when I wished for better things
just as the bad was spilling over
that day I found a four leaf clover
my luck, it turned around - moreover
I felt the joy good fortune brings
when I wished for better things
that day I found a four leaf clover

Alis Propiis Volat

The mystery is what tomorrow brings
if indeed it is guaranteed at all, and yet
she flies with her own wings

A certain uncertainty – a truth that rings
like a bell calling in sunset:
the mystery is what tomorrow brings

Fear tries to tie her wrists with strings
Still she controls her fate – you bet
She flies with her own wings

She is in love with the moments – just brief flings
The vanishing expected from the outset
The mystery is what tomorrow brings

She does not follow any maps; cries not for little things
They call her directionless; detached and yet
She flies with her own wings

She hasn't a care what the soothsayer sings
For horoscope prophets, even yesterday's regret
The mystery is what tomorrow brings
She flies with her own wings

In Perpetuum et Unum Diem

Forever and a day went by
when I'd lie there next to you
and we'd leave the curtains open
red sunrise to blue city moon

your love was aloof yet perilous
I would lose you in degrees
in your eyes I looked meritless
as I studied the debris

to find out what was broken
asking you for clues
but it was like I'd never spoken
and the words themselves were bruised

you never saw it coming when I left that May
roses on my doorstep, forever and a day

Imber

Stepped outside in my underwear
cool cup of half hearted coffee in hand
folded feet in faux wicker seat and

watched water like iridescent confetti
saturate old Queenslanders
attic windows with closed curtains

onomatopoeic thrum

tin rooftops with satellites asking
Saturn if it really does rain diamonds

finches rest on powerlines, ruffled wings

clouds in the wake of passing cars
rain like dust in a stampede

Imber like a hail of arrows
shot through the sky

meditative trance

imber
imber
imber

Post Meridiem
> *I want to touch your face as you sleep*

So I do

Ignoring the instinct that I shouldn't
and stroking, open palm, your sunkissed jaw
ignoring the familiarity of the gesture
and the wonder if I could ever tire of it

Sunlight washes the room aglow and is seeping
imperceptibly out of the day
you find my hand without searching,
clasp it close and you are still
so at ease while my heart beats wildly
in the cage you weren't supposed to reach

Underneath your eyelids lies
an expanse the colour of tropical reefs
so deep
I have to hold my breath
when you open them

Volume II: Memory

Millennial Paradox
Memories for a 2019 time capsule

These days we are better educated
        but can't remember how to write letters
Women have the right to vote
        but are underrepresented at the ballots
Never have we had such juicy options, ripe for picking
        but even Netflix has to tell us what to watch
How many people have missed the love of their life
on a busy street corner
        too busy swiping on Tinder?
Cigarettes are banned in countless places
        but city smog is blackening our lungs
        with fossil fuels
A kilo of fresh fruit is more expensive than fast food
        and there is more plastic in the ocean than fish
        more bullets in classrooms than children
We are more worldly than ever before
        but when bombs explode in Syria
        we change the channel
        close our borders
        build walls instead of walkways
Burn bridges and flags and entire towns and when
a teenage girl tells us our house is burning down
        we fly to outer space
        just to find a new home

There Were Frogs

Travelled to your hometown
of rain and frogs
and green
It took years but loss has a way
of bringing us home

They eyed me from afar as though
I was an accessory you'd paid for
traded whispers
               She's so young
this city girl precocious
pretentious, pretty in that city way
stealing our boy

At night we'd lie in the old
motel with all the heaters on and
the television with three channels
listening to the rain and I compulsively
checked my phone for reception
for some connection

I cried at the funeral because
it was sad but mostly because I had
a cold and was homesick and
didn't belong under your thumb
so much that your prints were all
over me

A bright green frog sprang across
my path – the first I'd ever seen
I stood in the rain and the grief with you
Watched a boy my age covered over with soil
Felt the ground shake beneath
my feet; a single thunderclap
from Heaven

Remembering the Dark Room

Sixth form.
Photography.
The dark room

a secret club with VIP access. 1100 girls
at school and only the smallest handful
allowed through that door

girls with cameras like extensions
of their arms. Girls who saw things
differently. Girls who felt at home
in the dark, redefining negatives

I remember my eyes adjusting. Obscured outlines
of school skirts. The way we'd measure development
times in song lyrics and dance moves.
How we laughed doubled over hard until
our sides hurt and our jaws ached

how sometimes we wondered if it was the fumes

and that time I swept my friend's tears from
her cheeks even though I couldn't see her
face. How I knew they were there
and pressed my fingertips to the salt

my vintage camera usually produced
blurred images and I would tell people
it was deliberate: that I saw the everyday
with a dreamlike quality

I said it until it was true.

Things I've Done in Houses

Etched my name into mantelpieces
Stayed awake all night listening
to another's breath
Broken up
Made up
Cried tears of regret over both
Smudged corners
Burned candles
Planted love spells in gardens
Held space when I had none of my own
Spent light years in front of mirrors
speaking hate to my reflection
Threw up drunken sorries and then realised
it was my own forgiveness I needed
Spilled rosé
and nail polish
and I love yous to people who didn't love me
Furnished empty corners and pretended
I was home

An Amalgamation of Memories

It's something about the way the light is falling
in soft shades of warm summer mandarin.
Something about the sleepy roads wide open yawn
stretching lazy sundaze into the distance.
Something about the mouth of the dried up old creek
and the scoop of pelicans synchronised swimming
in the lake full of floating paper flowers.
Something about the jangle of tram bells.

Something like a memory
of melting ice cream on hot afternoons
exploring tiny towns through camera lenses
trying to capture forever in cheap motel beds
and finding ripped polaroids of honeymoons jammed
behind the headboard. The way he looked at me as though
I was the strangest and most perplexing thing
he'd found to date.

There's a lot of Emotion Tied up in These Areas

There are no pictures on the wall,
sparse light as if the room itself
knows I need containment

I cannot see the screen so I imagine
what is seen and I am trained to master
an impassive gaze but I find hers so
unsettling

as she nudges my lifegiving gifts
with the tip of a camera, tunnelling, prodding
eyes on my internal artwork

searching for cracks in the canvas. She tells me
there's a lot of emotion tied up in these areas
and if it wasn't

for my tear-stung eyes I'd ask
if I could see my anguish

If it looks more ribbon
or rope.

Bird on the Wire

Bird on the wire
sings me awake;
this Earl Grey morning,
this weary Wednesday.

I watch it from my window,
and smile at its silhouette;
this enthusiastic alarm clock,
this noisy neighbour.

I promise to always notice
the extraordinary in the ordinary;
this Earl Grey morning,
This slow September.

My Scrubs are the Colour of Midnight

My scrubs are the colour of midnight.
I advertise inadvertently
a vegetarian café in Dunedin as my
calico bag bumps against my legs.
The satin floral scarf tied around one of
the handles floats in the breeze as though
it hasn't been a prisoner to that handle
for the last ten years.

Patients swim in and out of my mind.
I maintain a mental inventory
of medications, smiles, nods of empathy
and I think I should keep a tally
of how many tears I watch fall each week.

The half moon is a streetlight
illuminating my path to all the things
I look forward to in this moment:
a warm drink, a hot shower,
an electric blanket, retirement...
My millennial perspective reminds me
that only three of these things are attainable.
I adjust my goalposts accordingly.

My scrubs are the colour of midnight.
My heart is a harbour full of troubled ships.
I have frown lines of compassion, laugh lines
of encouragement; words of
hopefully,
hope.

The half moon is a streetlight,
guiding me home.

Kaikoura: November 14th 2016
7.8

Had I known when I went to bed that night,
I wouldn't have filled my glass of water so high.
I wouldn't have left things strewn on the floor.
I would've moved the precariously edge-dwelling ornament
on the bookshelf that I'd noticed hours earlier and thought,
    that'll break if there's an earthquake.

But the glass was full and the floor was messy
and the ornament waited on the edge.

And at 12:02am in pitch darkness I stumbled across
the shuddering floor as the house creaked and lurched,
rumbled and shook and I held tight to the doorway because
I've always had trouble standing up when it counts.

When the earthquake lost its power so had half the country
and in the dark we listened to an old battery operated radio as
midnight talkback hosts fielded crackly cellphone reports of
damage.
And the glass had tumbled over; water on the bedsheets,
up the wall, and the floor was even messier and the ornament was
broken at my feet and I went back to bed because
I know when I am beaten and
I counted the aftershocks.

In seven minutes there were three.

And at first light we saw the extent of the damage.
The skewed train tracks. The canyons in the roads.
The barnacles, clinging to the exposed seabed,
thrust up and out of the water as if it had decided
that it was no longer meant for the ocean
and wanted to see the sky.

Studying Stars

I knew a boy who was afraid of the day
when the sun burns out and I told him
it won't happen for five billion years
       we won't know
but fear makes things seem closer
than they really are

Someone saw the Southern Cross in my tea leaves,
said it's a constellation significant to me
and I tried to play nonchalant but all I could think
about was the time everything fell apart
and I followed it home

My grandfather studies the stars,
taught me how to call them by name,
showed me how to find Orion
in the night sky with his weapons but
I wanted to know what it was like
growing up when the world was at war.

He shrugged.

*You just learn early on to accept
that nothing is forever.*

The stars know it, too.

Below the Surface

I held the travel diary
of my grandfather's mother in my hands
ran my fingers across her words
hoped the DNA in my fingerprints
would unlock her voice

Notes from a ship on which
she sailed around the world some
fifty years ago
are all breakfasts and dinners
ports and sightseeing and
somewhere in the middle
a funeral

buried at sea
she had written and I wondered how
it must have felt to serve
witness to such a strange and eerie and
grave event

and how it must have felt as the ship
sailed away, knowing a lonely human
was still sinking
below the surface

By Any Other Name

I comment on the carpet
of daisies and she stares at me
perplexed, following my footsteps
along a road I've walked almost daily
almost all my life.
We, fledglings both:
she, a newcomer from Germany,
me, a naïve Kiwi on summer holidays.

What's daisy?

I think she's joking and then I see she's not
and I'm trying to pull words out of thin air
but they keep dematerialising
as I reach for them, so I reach instead
for a daisy,
hold it up for her to see, thinking maybe
they don't have them in Germany
but recognition dawns
on her face and she says a word
I've never heard and I ask

What's that?

She grins and I take a mental snapshot
of her blue eyes as she reaches
for the daisy;
holds it up for me to see.

The daisy cares not what its name is.
Just stretches its petals
and welcomes the sun.

Train Man

The man on the train is looking at me sideways
for a fraction too long and I try to slip into his
tightly laced shoes; to see what he sees:
a young woman,
rose quartz around her neck, an old key against
her breasts engraved with *fearless* on a chain.
Three days unwashed hair and a faraway gaze.
If he looks hard enough he could see my heart
beating against its cage;
quicksilver in my veins.
Underneath layers of clothes my thighs
sell you light.
The train rattles and we sway.
I don't know if he's hoping I move
out of his space
or in.

Cradling Perfection

Of all the gifts
that I've been graced with
the one that stands out today
is the year in which I had the supreme
privilege of holding new babies in my arms

I would cradle their tiny heads
instinctively sway
the safe harbour in a storm
whisper words of aroha
in broken Maori to those perfect
little Australians wishing them long
and healthy lives

that one day they might hear this
foreign language and wonder
why it seems vaguely familiar

Volume III: Hearts and Hurts

Riverside Love

Riverside,
the birds are heading home for the night,
sun nothing more than a pastel pink glow.
My book is open on my lap but my eyes
are on the young couple at the river's edge.

The bridge lights up purple,
the first bat of the evening swoops between trees.
My legs are itching from mosquito bites but my eyes
are on the way they lean towards each other.

He talks with his hands and she laughs
with her whole body and he responds
by running his talkative hands through his hair,
suddenly lost for words.

Between them, the moments run seamlessly together,
two disposable paper cups of liquid courage.
She wears a singlet with spaghetti straps
and no jacket, because love,
in its early stages,
can't feel the cold.

Matters of the Heart

When I learned that the average human heart
weighs 310 grams
I was surprised.

I didn't know there was such a thing as an average heart.

I knew about the cardiac muscle and its impulses,
its chambers full of blood and secrets.

I knew that broken heart syndrome was more
than poetic metaphor.

I knew the blue whale's heart is so large it can be heard
two miles away and I can only assume that's because it beats with
the depth of oceans.

The average human heart weighs 310 grams even when it's broken
and a select few get to hold it in their hands:
those who love us
those who save us
those who take an inventory of us
at the very end, and then the rescuers swoop in
to gently handle the grieving hearts left behind.

Curious, isn't it?
310 grams.
Such a flimsy weight for a vessel
that holds the essence of a life.

Instructions for the Builder

Build me a home from the ruins.
Repair the damage the years have done
and dress my raw-boned frame.
Tell me I'm still beautiful.
Fashion me from reclaimed materials
and sprinkle salt at all my thresholds.
Let the light stream in whenever I open up.
Remind me I'm a sun trap.
Let its rays warm me inside.
I've been a hollow shell for such a long time.
Breathe life into me.
Breathe life
into me.
Breathe.
Tell me when you look at me
you see more than wreckage.

True Colours

You changed a room.
Whenever you walked in it felt like
an open window on a summer day.
Did you know?

      (I never really told you)

how I learned to speak your favourite
colours and that time I saw you with her
crimson smile I cried
in tears of blue.

How I wished that just once
you'd catch sight of my pale blush
and yell
      oh! She is everything I'm looking for.

I would've shown you all of my colours.
But I never really found the courage.

When the World Ends I Will

I still haven't found a language
as at home on my tongue as your name.
Still haven't deciphered the labyrinth
of your fingerprints - they will dust me
for them like Venetian glass and if they ask
me whether I regret not telling you
that your hands left more than smudges
I'll say that I don't.

But I know when the world ends I will.

Love Me in Meadows

I want you to love me in meadows.
Whisper in the shell of my ear the songs
of babbling creeks – love me
like river rocks worn smooth with years
like a bee in the clover
like sunshine warms me inside out.
Love me wide open and evergreen
fingers full of grass
bramble-wreathed hair
wildflowers at my waist.

**On a Line from Henry Miller's Love Letter to Anais Nin
August 14th, 1932** *(Inspired by Anya Krugovoy Silver)*

I
You are full bloom flower
petals open bathed in sunshine
so close I could see each delicate
vein beneath paper fine flesh
pink and blushing sweet nectar
on my hummingbird tongue

I came away with pieces of you sticking to me

II
Skinnydipping with the fireflies
silver mooncharm water rolling wet
salacious golden skin so smooth
the night itself can't truly touch it
We float among the stars stung swollen
lips drink whatever passes through

I came away with pieces of you sticking to me

III

Love ruptures in bulletholes punctured
walls of hearts and homes the wreckage
is memories and fragmented what ifs
settling like dust on the floor

I came away with pieces of you sticking to me

Escape Routes

So it's like that, then.
I'm the dandelion fairy, floating on the breeze,
drifting weightlessly, airily, in search
of the horizon, to find out if its colours suit me.
I want to know if I can see past it.

Yours are the hands that grasp me,
raise me to your lips and make a wish.
Crumple me in your cupped palms;
ply me with demands.
I don't sail well on your breath,
have you noticed?

Pretend to set me free but only on your terms.
You can't pin me down though,
not really.
Your clumsy, calloused hands have cracks
between the fingers. Even the walls
of your heart are escapable
if I beat them down.

And so it becomes a game of two halves.
You can close every door.
I'll open the window.

Remember I had Wings

If you remember me for anything let it be this:
that I spent so much time looking up

at the sky, an imaginary crown of cloud lace and stars
atop my tousled head, wishing for wings;
that I might taste the blue.

That I was always in possession of an exit strategy
and your plans made me claustrophobic.

The many and varied ways in which I tried
to say I didn't want you.

How I wept when you clipped my wings.
How I knew I was meant for freedom.

The Weathering

I am the haven.
You are the storm.
I see your turmoil surging
across the horizon and I retreat
within myself, close off and seal
any sympathetic gaps in my spirit.
I will not allow you to flood me.
Outside, your hail lashes my exterior.

Whatever it Takes

I hung mirrors in the chambers
of my heart to make it look more spacious.
Tried to decorate it so the space
you once lived in didn't look quite so
empty.

I installed skylights in the atriums
and let the sun stream in,
filled the cracks with gold,
memorised all the different names
for the heart in the hopes
I'd eventually forget yours.

Whatever it takes.

Whatever.
It aches.

Pictures of You

Cleared out old memories today.
Found a few pictures of you
wearing that smile I knew.
The smile reserved for me.

Feels like yesterday and eternity
when I tried to build us a life
out of sticks and stones
broke all of my bones
bending over backwards for you.

I don't know whose hand you hold now,
or where in the world your heart is,
but I can tell you the best part is
when I tore those old pictures of you
in two,
I didn't feel a thing.

A Poem for You

Thanks for telling me all the ways that
I wasn't good enough
for all the comparisons to another
woman you used to love

You breathed in blunts and
spoke in sharps
not sure why you thought hurting me
was the way to my heart

Or did you want me at arms-length?
It's a little hard to say
treat 'em mean, keep 'em keen, right?
Watch me walk away

And when you buried yourself in me
I'd remind you I'm more temple than graveyard
You always said you wanted to be a poem
Baby,
now you are

Reflections on Sandcastles

In retrospect, it's crystal clear:
sand, under intense heat becomes glass,
fragile and transpicuous.
Glass, when dropped
by fumbling no good fingers
becomes a million fragments,
barbed and sorry.

It all makes sense:
I am a poor architect,
forever building castles
out of sand.

The Taste of an Apology

You poured your apologies into me
and they tasted like rose coloured wine
    smooth and sweet, filled with longing
and promises; soothing the darkened corners
of me, where I swept all those times you
    hurt my feelings; switched the light off
and pretended they didn't exist

I spent all night drunk on your sorries
only to wake the morning after
    with a sharp aftertaste
that smacked of regret

Orbit

At night it is Jupiter I search for
        all seventy nine moons in devotional orbit.

Under the milky spill of galaxy I savour
his flickering eye;
his turbulent storms.

I know a man who can read the night sky
like a map; in the shadowless nowhere,
navigating by the stars. He leaves behind
tiny constellations on my skin.

        I try not to orbit him.

Love Is...

Love is sensing a sore heart
and knowing the right language.
Love is *'wear a jacket, it's cold'*
and *'I saw this and thought of you.'*
Love is the letting go
and the coming back.
Love is love is love is love is love
is the space holding,
the life scaffolding,
Whispered forevers even though
there's no such thing.
Love is a smile that can light up a city.
Mountain peaks and ocean trenches
and good days, bad days, all the days.
Love is blind in its early stages
before it all becomes clear
and love is sitting with your fears,
within arms-reach but never feeding them.

Volume IV: Mind

Core Beliefs

I've come to realise that every child collects
assumptions, opinions, narratives, passed onto them
by people they look up to. Well-meaning people
who sometimes speak from ancient cobweb-covered hurts
they can't name.

And the children, they stuff all of these threads
into glass vessels labelled
Truth.

They carry them into adulthood.

It takes years to untangle them.

Anna was Here

Anna scuffed her sneakers on the doormat,
kicked them off, tiptoed inside.
Strung a hammock between my ribs
and made herself at home.
Anna sat on her perch,
questioned my worth,
told me there was too much of me
to love
and yet too little.
Anna put a lock on the fridge
and taught me how to count,
poisoned me from the inside out
and now I can't remember who I was.

Next Exit

I guess if I could conjure you, I'd ask
why you followed that exit sign.
Why you checked out at that moment
with no warning.
Why you took her with you.
We thought you were getting better.
We thought you were building new bridges,
new roads, we thought you were crawling
out of the tunnel, thought we could see the light
shining in your eyes, but maybe we were blind.
Maybe the darkness wasn't an illusion.
Maybe the light was.

Perspective

...Sometimes
I have to remind myself
that arranging my emotions is like
rearranging furniture;
which is to say,
if it doesn't sit well, take the time
to try angles that have been overlooked
and that could make all the difference.

What is Lost

Your words.
Your sense of self.
Your vision, gradually.
Your friends.
The light in your eyes
on this lonely day.
This quiet mourning.

Real Men Don't Cry

Tears escape
before he can stop them
which doesn't surprise me.
Grief has a knack for forcing
its way out, even when you try
to lock the door

Real men don't cry
he tells me, but I know they do
especially inside these four walls.
For a minute there I'd like to climb
inside his skin and learn what it is
to have to value hardness over
heartache

these men with their dry eyes.
I want to know the shame.
I want to know what it feels like
to drown in saltwater
from the inside

Let Your Eyes Adjust

When you finally see
that your waking hours are finite,
your dreams become paramount.
When you finally see
the gravity in your fears
you hitch them to the stars
and let them pull you free.
When you finally see
that privilege is a colour
you'll start to fight for every stripe
in the rainbow.
When you finally see
that every fall is broken at some point,
you'll land on your feet and start climbing.
All we have is this life; all we have is each other.
But it starts with ourselves,
when we finally see.

Thought Disorders

Echolalia:
    Is a parrot on your shoulder
                          On your shoulder

Word salad:
    a torrent of alphabet soup

Poverty of thought:
    is desert winds blowing

Derailment:
    is a train in an
        earthqu
                ake

Thought blocking:
    stops abruptly as the entire -

Perseveration:
    loves to repeat for no reason no
    reason no
    reason

Flight of ideas:
    is a gulp of swallows, swooping
    around in the brain

Clang associations:
> vibrations
>> consternations
>>> situations
>>>> fabrications

Tangentiality:
> never follows the signposted path
> and

Circumstantiality:
> always takes the long way around

Working in the Dark

I wade through the dark for a living;
spend my hours helping people
find the light.

I thought I was enlightened.

But when someone hypothesized
that those who work in the dark see everything,
suddenly all I had were questions.

Later that night, I tested the theory.
Outside on the still hot summer concrete I lay
beneath the night sky, looking for answers.

Above me, the moon, the stars,
and all my truths
hung in the balance.

Skylight

Tell me about this darkness that you're feeling
I'll stand right by your side in it – I won't run
You'll see the light inside you is revealing
It's the dawn that permeates when night is done
The new day brings a second chance for healing
Sacred light not guaranteed to everyone
So the next time your sky becomes a ceiling
Build a skylight and remember you're the sun

Life Line

Somewhere along the line I started to keep track
of all the different lines the skin can carry.
You are lined with silver and survival and I know this
for certain because when I look at you I see
the lines of resilience, and I don't tell you enough
but my favourite part of you is the ravine that runs
deep and forked across the landscape of your palm.

You think you're empty handed yet
you're holding infinite hope.

Volume V: Twenty Twenty

Season of Flames

It is the beginning of bushfire season
and this, the worst on record.
We go about our days in a haze,
seeping across the hills from small towns ablaze.
Ashen faces on the six o'clock news
charcoal trees.
Cinders in our morning coffees
settling on our lungs, we gaze
at the sun's aura and wish for rain.
Black smoke tears of summer
fury in our eyes.
Come early evening there is no rest
for those battling in the bushfire zones.
Above us the sky is a canvas painted
the colour of burning homes.

2020

Day one of 2020 and fires are still burning
charred ruins still smoking, people still fighting
still running
still dying

here is what I know:
in the face of trauma it is difficult
to differentiate between a moment
and an eternity

this shall pass and in the smouldering
we will scatter seedlings
reforesting the land, learning its wisdom

and we will salvage hope
and tend our own gardens
fashioning a life from the wreckage

we too are here to grow

The Weight of Smoke and Darkness

The dark is blinding.
String lights a dim glimmer,
candles flicker and I gaze
into the flame.
Everything is normal but
nothing's the same.

Inside, the news is a muffled murmur.
I don't need to hear it.
Smoke strangles me; two hands
around my throat, filling my chest
cavity. If my eyes are stinging at least
I know I'm alive.

I carry stories of friends losing
loved ones in past infernos.
Stories whispered to me in the middle
of the night or recounted over
cups of tea.

The weight of them is heavy just now.

I extinguish the candles, licked fingers
to the wick. Wish for rain.
In the corner, the chandelier made
from seashells shivers like old bones.

The Language of a State of Emergency

I once read a book about Australian bushfires,
set in rural Victoria, all dry grass and
parched branches.

So it was from third or fourth hand wisdom
that I learned the traditional practice
of controlled burns; the respectfully wary
coexistence of humans, the earth
and Australia's unforgiving climate.

Fast forward twelve years.
The climate has changed exponentially
and I'm living in this country under
smoke choked furnace glow black as night skies.

It is January but the embers continue
to rain down on towns and we rem-ember
the lost, shed tears from fire hoses
but it's not enough.

      It's not enough.

I know a lot more these days.
Mostly about language.
For example, the most chilling sentence
goes exactly like this:

> *It is too late to leave.*
> *It is too late to leave.*
> *It is too late to leave.*

Seek shelter.

Things that are Missing from Me
for New Zealand

Oceans of long grass for wading,
rolling hills for conquering,
viewing platforms at the top
for marvelling,
Sea fog
creeping in overnight, waking up
underneath an extra blanket and
the heady fragrance of chimney smoke
for warming mornings,
chipping ice from the windscreen
with numb fingers and pyjama clad
dancing in the eerie hush of
midnight snow.

It's normal in times of crisis,
the textbooks told me so

This yearning for the familiar;
for all the things we used to know.

(It's still so lonely though.)

Chrysalism

I live under a flight path
frequently deafened by the roar
of manmade birds but
as of today the sky highway is
quiet
long stretches of empty like
the dusty desert roads
between Arizona
and California

Instead of aeroplanes
butterflies
spread their wings and dance
outside, spanning the social distance
between us

This chrysalism
we find ourselves in is both
necessary and grave
We bite our nails behind
closed doors.

We wait.

I Stay Home

for the frail
and the innocent
for those under the poverty line
and above it
for the young
and the restless
for those aware of their mortality
and those who feel invincible

I stay home
for the worried masses
for the ignorant
and those with world-weary
weighted shoulders
for the healers
and the healing
and the ones with age old wounds

I stay home
for the balcony chorus
for the window applauders
for the ones who welcome solitude
and the ones who fear it

Lauren Kaeli Baker

I stay home
for the lungs of the world
and hearts united

I stay home
for you

Wild Chamomile

Feels like yesterday
when flames swallowed trees swallowed lives
swallowed picket fence dreams
but in real time this matchbox nation regenerates,
medicinal trees heal in the breeze and now
is the season of wild chamomile unbridled.

I saw some today at the steps of the mosque
where I left flowers just over a year ago
(or yesterday) when white privileged bullets
punctured prayers punctured lives punctured
picket fence dreams.

In real time people on the street wear masks,
foodies line up for brunch at old favourites
where morning mimosas and
macchiatos are sipped in time limited increments.
Hand sanitiser on tables in place of flowers and candles
and lines indicate where to stand as though
we are all pretending here and our planet is a stage.

The wild chamomile is going to seed.
The world is heavy with grief.

Weaving

The streets are mostly empty,
flowers bloom for no one but themselves,
leaves drift from sun-dappled canopies.
The dead collect on the ground
and the orb spiders keep on weaving

The streets are mostly empty,
leaves move from green to red
to yellow with seasonal change.
The dead skitter ghostly along the ground
and the orb spiders keep on weaving

The streets are mostly empty,
threads of conversation caught from windows,
the leaves, they whisper too.
The dead rest quietly wherever they fall
and the orb spiders keep on weaving

The streets are mostly empty,
abandoned playgrounds overgrown,
leaves leave branches bereft.
The dead multiply at an alarming rate
and the orb spiders keep on weaving

Hipster Breakup in Quarantine

We watch art house movies,
nearly all of them
ominous

sit apart, plaintive questions,
asking
do we have to keep going?
Ask yourself if you need more
        hours

Evening shadows joy
across the city, spills
from stoops, windows, rooftops
for all
who cannot heal

The Shelter and the Distance

This past month, sheltering
seems like eternity.
Even partial, we are many.
A suspended release of
pieces in pursuit of
electrifying feats of
lifelong distance

What Matters is All of Us

In the evenings I'm humbled.
Every day the nervous energy
is amplified, overwhelming,
not just at the end

A deep address:
>*We all matter.*
>*All of us do.*
>*We will be there.*
>*You will not be alone.*

Pandemic

Everything changed, suddenly
catastrophe,
a horrible portent of devastation.
Photographs show scenes
of calamity
of absence
of empty.
A post-apocalyptic void.

A Spell to End the Pandemic

Doors must be closed.
Hands washed
under soapy water for
thirty seconds,
no less. Repeat.
Do not hold hands.
The spell only works
with
d i s t a n c e

The transformation
happens as parents teach
their children everything
they know and love is found
to be communicated without
hands

Hospitals work their magic

Incantations whispered
on bended knees,
at bedsides, in curtained
darkness, at rainy windows,
in havens
and in cages
work their magic

And the world breathes
a collective sigh and
the doors are flung open
on rusted hinges and
the people spill
into the streets

Life goes on
once they pause for a spell

Makes A Mockery

The pandemic mocked us.
Confronting and enforcing
fears
concentrated hospitals
prepared to take hundreds.

You get worse.

I live.

Volume VI: The After

To the Patron Saint of Staying In
after Chelsea Coreen

Prayed to you tonight.
Barefoot, braless prayer, the kind
that doesn't observe ceremony but
rather settles in comfortably with some
kind of scripture, usually a mystery novel
and on my tongue full bodied chocolate melts
like wax on candles that smell
like home.
Wine in my glass and holy water in the shower.
O, patron saint of sunsets
from the kitchen window,
Netflix-are-you-still-there messages,
cellphone silenced early nights,
stay in with me.

Op Shop, 1985
after Majella Cullinane

Doorbells chime
        enter shop and meditative state
at once, traipse worn lino floor
with mindful purpose

you are here
        in this memory laden store full of
haunted objects and lived in denims
        you are here
with armloads of your own haunting

your reptile skins
        you are shedding yourself, you are
letting go
        of your ghosts and all the pieces of you
best left behind

Doorbells chime
        step into the present, shake off
lingering doubts, you are here.
        The morning warm sun leaks
into new skin, sinks into old bones

Demeter
after Carol Ann Duffy

I wake one day and I know she has gone.
Slipped away undercover of darkness
as though she is the thief and not
the treasure stolen

I am alone again in my cold stone winter room,
abandoned crucifixes and pomegranate
seeds scattered blood red, the colour
of her lips as he comes closer

She has always been terrible at goodbyes.
Just yesterday she was drawing lotus flowers
blooming in the margins; my eternal spring

Today she has left me a single line
scrawled in pomegranate juice:
the sin is not so bad.

Tea
after Leila Chatti

My great grandmother harvested rosehips.
Steeped them into tea, to salve.
Swallowed some secret sadness
no one knew of.

Her daughter; my grandmother
cannot bear the smell of tea, says
it reminds her of her nursing days
and all the hurt she couldn't heal.

She calls the tea my grandfather drinks
water bewitched. She says it's because of the weak
alchemy of leaf to water but I always thought
it was because the women in my family –
the tea makers, were witches.

My mother barely drinks the stuff, says
it reminds her of addicts she once knew. Remembers
the tremulous clang of china cup to saucer; remembers
the chips and the spills and the relapse.

My first memory of tea is as replacement
to poison, cooling on my neighbour's table as he lay
bleeding on the floor.

These days I steep almond milk on stovetop,
star anise and cinnamon, grated ginger for the soul.
I know there is magic in this ritual, I know
my lips to the cup cast a spell.

When the psychic read my leaves he saw remnants
of my genetic make up, which is to say,
poetry
and constellations.

Dark Sonnet
 after Neil Gaiman

Storm cellar, wretched lightless room
where you once held me through the storm
is but a memory of you entombed
though in my mind you are frayed and worn

I'd stand in the gale, let it lift me from the ground
if only I had no fears
and if only the wind had a Lost and Found
if only it could strip away years

Here in this shelter of shadows I dwell
you left me here alone
and love is a cyclone the poets know well:
it leaves wreckage where it's blown

All those candles I lit so you could see in the dark
I didn't know you were blind to me from the start

Burning the Old Year
after Naomi Shihab Nye

New Years Eve.
This time last year half the country was on fire
and today is the last day of the last ember and this year
has been so heavy. This year grabbed us by the throat

and made sure we couldn't breathe. This year we fought
to survive, this year love meant distance meant closed doors
meant forfeiting goodbyes. This year

the flames are mostly metaphorical and still
to burn it seems too grave

an act, despite the grief and so
I put on my favourite dress, prepare a stick of holy wood
- smudge every corner of my soul. Bake cookies for two

and eat them alone and think in some ways
nothing has changed and in some ways
everything has.

Prayer to Persephone
after Edna St Vincent Millay

Persephone,
I want to know what he whispers to make you come every winter
To trade waterfall for Styx, meadows for chains,
shaded sycamore languorous limbs for fiery throne
      what is it about him?

And when you get there I want to know
do you press yourself to the floors like sorrow?
Or do you slip between his sheets like longing?
Is that red wine in your chalice or...?

      Are you never hungry there?
      Are you always?

Do you ever laugh that you have everybody fooled?

Persephone,
I wish you would tell me all your secrets.

Like the exact bathwater ratio of salt to roses
to lull them into thinking you're pristine.

Or perhaps
how to crush cherry blossom petals into cheekbones
to look blameless.

Dandelion Insomnia
after Ada Limon

What colours do you dream in
while I lie here next to you encased in nothing
but witching hour ink?

You sleep soundly, full of soft breath
and eyelash wishes, folded into yourself
sweetly like California Poppies close
their petals to the moon

Beside you I am a dandelion insomniac
questioning how it is that I can be primary colour
stereotype one minute, only to fragment
into broken wishes the next

In the earliest of hours I rebuild
so when you wake in the palm of
the gracious dawn you notice nothing
more than leftover dust on my eyelashes

The Hurt Child
after Margaret Atwood

The hurt child begins as plasticine -
pliable and covered in thumbprints from
careless hands. It begins as a susceptible host
to infectious pathogens from profound parental
wounds

and the thumbprints, they turn into wounds
themselves and they fester and seep
family narratives and they keep the hurt child
up at night not realising that the monster it fears
is inside it

and the hurt child explodes like a lit match
in a coal mine - a firestorm of fists and flailing
legs and it howls every vicious word

ever said to it in anger and your own skin
must be strong enough to withstand
the lacerations

Lauren Kaeli Baker

The hurt child is red faced and spitting
and its screams split the earth
and its tears flood the room
and its fears pierce the heavens

and it will keep bleeding from
hand-me-down wounds too deep
for it to carry and you will never
have a band-aid big enough

An Exercise in Love
after Diane Di Prima

My friend comes to my door
with rum and coke and
sometimes his
laundry

He brings me music, weaves me stories
I bring him hours of escape; of softness
he picks up my candles, incense sticks
runs his fingers over everything
as though I live in an art gallery
and I am myself
a work of
art

We explore vastness and depths
without leaving my room
he comes from a distant land and I meet him
- borrow his tongue and learn
how to say filthy words in
holy language

When daylight comes I wonder
if he was just a dream

Volume VII: The Blackout

Blackout

City of night
and there, hope repeated.
We circled
and shone, strange ghosts
of people.
Those days breathed
and cried
and uttered.
I fell towards the first
light I saw.

The Trip

Sparsely furnished minutes
dropping on the fourth floor :
thrill of trips unambitious
dark watchful eye intent

      Wizard of Oz

is dreamscape
vivid, heartfelt and good
Home stretches
to flat horizon
real life unreal ;
      mild as bathwater

Flying monkeys darken
department store windows

The Darkest Blackout

How cruel;
mistaken humanity and nothing else

hope to wallow in the divinity -
       long tale of tears

suffer your woes and beseech
the apocalypse

       (no one is secure)

Extraordinary Ordinary

I came to like
ordinariness,
the same thing over;
the flawed immediate.
I wanted infinite,
arrow shoots,
the colour of July rain.

Someone Once Said I Was Otherworldly

Disheveled in the midst
of ghostly spirit
lovely lips to golden skin
in moonlight gauze magic

She is morning, vanished
beneath midnight awry
graceful and close – ask:

Are you of this world?

First

Immediate, new and then
perhaps a little strange.
She had never known,
somehow.

Solemn cheeks burn fearful,
sweet and frosted shock.

Her waist, creased.
His coat, dusty.

Wonders

Do you hear the angels laugh?
    (Breath of wide-eyed awe)

Forget everything you know –

Discover power in the earth
    (love the sky)

Find existence in forever

Heartcure

Take on a life mixed with roses,
tea,
simmer for deep love.
Amulet apples in the evenings
Say : heartcure
Say : cinnamon, bayberry, thyme
combination chamomile
raspberry mornings
courage
to discover yourself

Gratitudes: For Those Who Write and Inspire

Thank you to all of the brilliant poets in the Instagram community, who provided inspiration for many of the poems in this collection:
@skyler.celeste.poetry
@the_colourofhope
@chimenkouri,
@kristianamst
@paulaklewisgamble
@asm.poetry
@m_is_for_marigold
@comrade_david_writes,
@amykaypoetry
@poemsandpeonies
@blushing_poetry
@a.j.butler.poetry

Thank you also, to the poets I've written poems after:
Anya Krugovoy Silva,
Chelsea Coreen,
Majella Cullinane,
Carol Ann Duffy,
Neil Gaiman, Leila Chatti,
Naomi Shihab Nye,
Edna St Vincent Millay,
Ada Limon,
Diane Di Prima,
and Margaret Atwood

Lastly, thank you to Austie Baird, for patiently battling time zones and distance, creating an incredibly beautiful cover design, and putting the entire collection you've just read together.

Have you enjoyed these works by Lauren Kaeli Baker?

To find more by this author please visit her Instagram:
@sweetbriar_june

You can also find her work in the following books:
Solace: Poetry of Nature (2020)
Notes from Sweet Briar (2019)

Available on Amazon!

www.ingramcontent.com/pod-product-compliance
Lightning Source LLC
LaVergne TN
LVHW041229080426
835508LV00011B/1122